TRADITIONAL MASQUERADE OF SAINT LUCIA

Characters and Costumes, Music and Dances, Chants and Rituals

by June Frederick

Featuring artwork from Alwyn St. Omer and Jonathan Guy-Gladding

All rights reserved. For information about permission to reproduce selections from the book or to arrange an author visit for your school, contact CaribbeanReads Publishing, P. O. Box 7321, Fairfax Station, VA 22039 or info@caribbeanreads.com.

Text copyright 2020 June Frederick

Acknowledgements:

Paintings: Front and back cover, Masqueraders on title page, and Page 8 by Alwyn St. Omer. Masquerade band on title page and pages 2, 3, 4, 5, 6, 8, 12, 13, and 14 by Jonathan Gladding.

Resource persons: Mr. Eric Branford and Gregor Williams St. Lucian Historians, Hazel Simmonds-McDonald, Dr. Winston Philgence, Michelle Theobalds, YIA Masqueraders of the Youth in Arts (YIA) Theatre Company.

Resource material: "Piti Kon Nou Piti," children's activity book with DVD on the Traditional Masquerade of St. Lucia and the resource persons with information from an FRC/UNESCO project on the Revitalization of Traditional Masquerade.

Photographs: Pages 21 and 22 courtesy of Ted Sandiford.

Pages 8, 9, 11, 16, and 18 supplied by the author, June Frederick.

CaribbeanReads Publishing
First Edition
All rights reserved.
Printed in the USA
ISBN: 978-1-953747-02-0 paperback

DEDICATION

To the late Mr. Gisson, Mr. Monterro, Athenatius LaBorde, Cyril "Slade" Mitchell, and all other Masquerade performers and musicians who have gone before us.

To Niger Nestor, Cuthbert Popo, and others who continue to work tirelessly with the upcoming generation to teach our Masquerade music and rhythms.

To Barry George and the Silver Shadows Dance Academy for staging the traditions for over 30 years.

To the KiddiCrew.com kids who participated in my first attempt to put Masquerade back on the streets of Castries and to the YIA Masqueraders whose interest and excitement to perform keep my passion going and the tradition alive.

To my husband Bobby for his support in many more ways than one, and to my precious children, Gabriele, Omari, Darcel, and Kareem, whose interest in and excitement for the traditions continue to inspire me.

And to my precious parents, Winville and Thelma King, for teaching me to love our country's culture and traditions.

TABLE OF CONTENTS

Introduction 1

Chapter 1: Characters, Music, and Dances 2

Chapter 2: The Music of the Masquerade 6

Chapter 3: The Movements of the Masquerade 8

Chapter 4: The Characters 12

Chapter 5: The Chants 15

Chapter 6: The Rituals 17

Chapter 7: Interesting Facts 19

About the Author 20

About the Artists 22

INTRODUCTION

BACKGROUND AND HISTORY

St. Lucia's Traditional Masquerade is an exciting cultural artform performed during our Christmas Season. It comprises costumed characters patterned off St. Lucia's rich history.

The traditional time for Saint Lucia's Masquerade is December 13th to January 2nd. Saint Lucia is the only Windward Island where Masquerade is performed at Christmas; in the other islands, Masquerade is part of the Carnival tradition.

Historically, St. Lucia's Masquerade is linked to the moonlight dances during the times of African slavery in St. Lucia when, according to St. Lucian historian Eric Branford, enslaved people would go from house to house, dancing and singing to the accompaniment of musical instruments. After emancipation, this practice continued as community performances in the rural areas. Later on, as persons migrated to the capital Castries to work, they performed on the streets for the persons with whom they worked and earned income from money thrown to them by onlookers in balconies and standing on the side of the road.

There are distinct influences from European and African cultures in the Masquerade characters, dances, musical instruments, costumes, costume names, and language of chants. The major root of our Masquerade comes from West Africa with known sources from the Yoruba and Kalabari traditions of the Rivers state in Nigeria. These include ancient and religious rituals in which characters wear the masks of deities, and ancestral spirits are represented in animal and plant characters and in stilt walkers or Moko Jumbies.

The Masqueraders perform to the different rhythms of African and European instruments including the drums, flute, and shak-shak. Some wear brightly-coloured costumes with cone-shaped hats and others depict animal and plant characters. These Masquerade traditions can be found in other Caribbean islands which have similar historical influences.

In St. Lucia, there are two groups of Masqueraders. One group dances to the music of the masquerade band. The other group has no musical accompaniment, but instead, moves to the rhythms of chants, and performs death and resurrection rituals on the street. The latter group comes out only at Christmas but the group that dances to the music of the traditional masquerade band performs all year round.

Early Masquerade performers were all male, role-playing as women when needed. Nowadays, females perform most of the dances, but the group that moves to the rhythm of chants remains predominantly male with the possibility of the inclusion of one female character.

CHARACTERS, MUSIC, DANCES

Excerpt from Roderick Walcott's "Papa Diable, the Devil at Christmas:"

"...On Christmas Day,
The country bands would come
With flute
And drum
And some shak-shak player
From very far away

Their dancers had on women's clothes,
With tall hats in crepe paper;
Bearing such names as "Pay Bannann,"
"Chouval Bwa," and "Uncle Sam."

The characters who dance to the music of the Masquerade are as follows:

MASQUERADE DANCERS

They wear brightly-coloured dresses with an enamel cup tied round the waist, white pantaloons, and cone-shaped hats brightly adorned with coloured crepe paper (or strips of cloth). As both females and males form this group, the male dancers cover their faces with masks or brightly-coloured cloth.

PAY BANNANN

Pronounced: Pie Banan
Translation: Banana leaves

This character dresses in long pants and a long-sleeved shirt covered with dried banana leaves and ties his/her head with a brightly-coloured or madras cloth. The face may also be covered with cloth or a wire mask.

Males and females wear this costume. According to local myth, this character was the first ever to be performed on the street by a female. Up until then, only males performed, role-playing as females in most instances. That female dancer was a banana farmer who hid her identity by covering her clothes with dried banana leaves and masking her face. She performed for years before anyone realized that she was female.

Following our African traditions, Masquerade characters include a plant and animal character as there is a strong belief that animals and plants are connected to the ancestral spirit world and have to be honoured.

Traditional Masquerade of Saint Lucia

CHOUVAL BWA

Pronounced: Shooval Bwa
Translation: Wooden Horse

A wooden or PVC frame covered by a large skirt with a horse's head and tail forms the main part of this costume. The performer fits into the frame wearing a peasant blouse, pants, and a head tie.

According to local myth, this costume came about as a result of a search for something to mimic a horse. The frame was taken from the local wooden Merry-Go-Round and dressed up accordingly. This character also follows the African tradition of honouring the ancestral spirits living in animals.

Chapter 1

UNCLE SAM AND SERAPHINA

These are stilt walkers or Moko Jumbies who were introduced into the street parade in the mid 20th century when farmers were recruited from St. Lucia to work on plantations in the United States. It is said that they returned home with three things: short-wave radio, Country & Western music and dance, and the stilt walker: Uncle Sam. The character, Seraphina, his St. Lucian wife was then created.

Uncle Sam wears a costume decorated with stars and stripes and a black top hat. His wife, Seraphina, wears a floral dress strategically stuffed to create a very large bosom and a large wide-brimmed hat.

Masqueraders usually make money by picking up whatever is thrown on to the street by the crowd. As Uncle Sam and Seraphina are on stilts, they cannot collect money from the street, so they rely on persons to put money in their hats as they bend towards them. This strategy worked very well in the early days, when all festivities happened around the Columbus Square (since renamed the Derek Walcott Square). The houses there were tall with balconies, and employers and guests would throw coins to performers. It was also easy for these tall characters to take off their hats to collect the money from the onlookers in the tall balconies.

On their website nccctt.org, the National Carnival Commission of Trinidad and Tobago writes that the "Moko Jumbie derives its name from West African tradition. The 'Moko' is an Orisha (God) of Retribution. The term 'Jumbie' [spirit] was added post-slavery. The Moko Jumbie was regarded as a protector whose towering height made it easier to see evil before ordinary men."

In an article entitled "The Moko Jumbie: A cultural Icon" on the "Go to St. Croix" blog, reports that the "presence [of moko jumbies] was an important part of African religious ceremonies as well as to the rites of passage when a boy is recognized as a man and a girl as a woman. Many African tribes believed that Moko Jumbies acted as the spiritual seers and protectors of the village."

5

THE MUSIC OF THE MASQUERADE BAND

THE INSTRUMENTS

The Masquerade Band is made of the following instruments:

THE SNARE DRUM

This is a modern drum that has replaced the Kettle drum. The rolls of this drum are unique to the Masquerade and known to very few.

THE KETTLE DRUM

This was originally the African Bwa. It is also called the Kettle drum, but is different in shape and size from the European kettle drum.

THE FLUTE

The flute used in masquerade music was traditionally made of bamboo, but this has now been replaced by the penny whistle in C. Music Recorders can also be used as they both have the same tone as the traditional bamboo flute.

THE BASS DRUM

This can either be a traditional drum made of goat skin and wooden rum barrels or a modern bass drum.

THE SHAK-SHAK

This percussion instrument is patterned after the shakers and rattles of West African instruments traditionally used in religious ceremonies. Our local shak-shak is made from a long tin filled with seeds. It has a distinct rhythm that takes time to master, and when on the street, the player has to have considerable stamina to keep up with performances.

Chapter 2

THE MUSIC

There are three distinct rhythms for the Masquerade performance: the March, the Quick Tempo, and the Waltz.

THE MARCH

The March is used to introduce the Masquerade dancers who comically exaggerate classic march steps and form patterns on the road. The drummer hits the snare drum four times to begin the next sequence which is the Quick Tempo.

QUICK TEMPO

The dances that accompany this music have patterns that can be used in any sequence with specific steps that have been named by the YIA Masqueraders. After performing these dance patterns, the dancers freestyle and interact with onlookers to the rhythm of the Quick Tempo until the music stops.

The Pay Bannann and Masquerade dancers also perform bamboo dancing to the Quick Tempo. Two bamboo poles are used. They are controlled by four players and the dancers perform comic movements on them while trying to maintain their balance.

THE WALTZ

In order to catch their breath after the exertion of the Quick Tempo, the Band plays a waltz. Dancers perform a drunken walk and tilt their heads from side to side thus showing off the pretty cone-shaped hats. The drummer hits the kettle drum four times to restart the Quick Tempo sequence.

THE MOVEMENTS OF THE MASQUERADE

SLOW MOVEMENTS (WALTZ)

Tèt Womyé

Pronounced: Tet WomyayMeaning: Rum Head

This is a slow forward movement with the dancer bending forward, swaying, and pulling their upper body up while moving their head from left to right. This is repeated until the music changes rhythm.

This movement is used to catch the performer's breath after the quick movements and to show off the beautiful cone-shaped hats.

Dance March

This is a comical dance movement to a marching rhythm: Left, right, left, right with comical waist ("wining") movements. Dancers also form marching patterns as part of their March routines.

This movement is used to announce the Masqueraders.

QUICK MOVEMENTS

Following the march or the slow music, the snare drummer hits the drum four times. This signals the beginning of the quick movements which usually begin with the Pyé Chó.

Pyé Chó

Pronounced: Peeay Show   Meaning: Hot Foot

For this movement, the performers on single time, jump and stretch out the right foot ending on the heel, jump and stretch out the left foot ending on the heel, repeat alternately four times and then repeat the movements on double time for eight counts. Hands are on the waist.

Had Dèyè

Pronounced: Had Dehyeh   Meaning: Dress behind

Performers twist their bodies from side to side in a three-step movement with their skirts held at their back at their waist. This movement usually comes in between the quick movements.

Had Dwèt ek Goch

Pronounced: Had Dwet ek Goach   Meaning: Dress Right and left

Performers make a forward dance movement while swirling their skirts from left and right in a rhythm. This movement also comes in between the quick movements and gives performers a breather

Zèl Poul or The Flapper

Pronounced: Zell Pool   Meaning: Chicken Wing

Performers bend their arms at the elbow and flap arms like wings while moving to the right, crossing their feet for four counts finishing on the heel, then to the left with same movement four times. They repeat this movement four times with a turn for four counts first to the right then to the left.

Wimen Anba or Wine Down

Pronounced: Weemeh Uhba   Meaning: Wine Down

This is a full body movement. For a count of eight, performers move arms, shoulders, and waist in a downward movement, bending knees into a squat position for a count of eight.

Bosi or Humpback

Pronounced: Boe-see   Meaning: Humpback

The Wimen Anba flows into this movement. From the squat position, performers put the left knee down then the right knee, bring the right hand from the back, over the head to the ground and then the left hand over the head to the ground in an all fours position.

Facing front for four counts, performers flex and release the back (one flex and one release is considered one count), then with a quick clap of the hands the performers change their hand placement and are now facing right, flex and release, clap, face the left, flex and release, clap and back to the front.

Soukwé Aho or The Shimmy

Pronounced: Sookway Ahoe   Meaning: High Shake

The *Bósi* or Humpback flows into this movement. From the all fours position, performers lift the upper body with hands spread out shoulder high and shimmy the upper chest and arms four times to the front, back to the all fours position, to the right and back to the front, left and back to the front each time coming down to the all fours position.

Moulavan or The Windmill

Pronounced: Moolavuh   Meaning: The Windmill

Following the Shimmy, female performers "wine up" to a standing position for eight counts. They then make quick shuffling steps with arms in a circular motion moving their bodies four counts to the right and four counts to the left, repeating four times on each side. Total count of sixteen.

Following the Shimmy, and while the female dancers are doing the Moulavan or Windmill, Pay Bannann characters lie on their backs with both legs up in the air, put hands in between their legs and shimmy both hands and legs in between for a count of eight then "wine up" to a standing position. Total count of sixteen.

Mi Mwen or Look Me

Pronounced: Me Mweh   Meaning: Here am I

The skirt is bunched up and held with the both hands in front of the performer. They bend their knees forward and turn their body to the right with the hands making an upward movement with the skirt. This is repeated on each side for eight counts.

Panché Douvan èk Bali Koul Pyé or Forward and Kick

Pronounced:
    Puhshay doovuh ek balee cool Peeyay   Meaning: Bend forward and kick

The performers begin upright and then move, bending forward with the right arm to the right leg and ending with a short kick with left leg and left arm lifting straight up above the head. This is done on alternate sides for a count of four.

Soté Lavé or Jump and Wash

Pronounced: Soetay lavay   Meaning: Jump and Wash

Performer holds skirt in front with two hands, then makes short quick jumps landing with bent knees. While jumping, the performer makes a motion with their hands as if washing the skirt. This is repeated for eight counts.

Gadé Dèyè or Rude Gyal 1

Pronounced: Gaday Dehyeh   Meaning: Look behind

The body is bent forward and the right leg is moved in four short steps backwards with the hand and head following. On the fourth step the right hand is brought around and hits the bottom with a short tap. This is then done on the left side and repeated four times on alternate sides.

Jouké or Jook

Pronounced: Jookay   Meaning: Jook

The body twists from side to side with both legs bent at the knee while both arms move in the opposite direction crossing in front of the body for three counts. On the fourth count, the performer bends knees up and pulls both hands down to the knees while slightly tilting body back shouting Yé with this move…this is done four times alternately on the left and right.

Maté Wimen or Bend and Wine

Pronounced: Matay Weemeh   Meaning: Bend over and wine

Performers begin in an upright position. Bend body forward from the waist, bend the right leg up at the knee, move to the right, moving the bottom from side to side for a count of four…this is repeated four times moving to the right, four times moving to the left with the leg lift leading the movement – right leg body moves to the right, left leg body moves to the left.

These are the basic movements that can be used in any order for street performances and adapted for stage performances.

Spontaneous Movement

Dancers perform freestyle and also take members of the audience to dance with them.

THE CHARACTERS

These are characters that move only to the rhythm of chants and perform death and resurrection rituals. They do not dance to the music of the Masquerade Band and are all males.

PAPA DJAB OR TOES

Excerpts from Roderick Walcott's "Papa Diable, the Devil at Christmas"

"So let me talk of Papa Djab
The Devil at Christmas time;
A comic infidel
Vacationing from Hell
Out of season and out of place
A laughing stock for the human race."

"... a man all dressed in red
And wearing sisal for a beard
Like Father Christmas from the dead!"

This character is similar to portrayals of Eshu, the trickster God of the Yoruba, and the European Father Christmas.

It is said that Papa Djab is the slaves' rebellious response to the evil Europeans' Father Christmas. Like Father Christmas he wears an all red jump suit, his face is painted white with a white sisal beard; he wears white gloves and black shoes (or is barefooted). He has horns at the top of his head patterned off the trickster God, Eshu, and around his waist he carries a red pouch for money. As his followers collect money they put it in the pouch which assumes a phallic form.

In his hand he carries a staff, the top of which is shaped like four fingers. He also wears a long tail which ends in an arrow point.

He is King of the Masquerade and orders his followers to do his bidding, just as the white planters ordered the slaves to do their bidding; he instils fear in both adults and children but is a mischievous, and not an evil devil.

Chapter 4

ACROBAT

Excerpt from Roderick Walcott's "Papa Diable, the Devil at Christmas:"

"His right hand in black and yellow
Was an extremely lively fellow.
They call him Acrobat by name.
He tried to steal his master's fame"

Acrobat dresses in a black and yellow shirt with black tights. His costume mimics that of the European court jester, complete with the black and yellow court jester's hat. His face is painted, half-yellow, half-white. These two colours portray his ability to lead the enslaved blacks into trouble while challenging the planter as the powerful man in charge.

He shows off his acrobatic skills with flips and jumps on the street and his main role is to try to usurp Papa Djab's role by stealing his pouch of money and making advances on his wife, Mary Anset. His actions incite both of the rituals on the street.

TI DJABS OR DJABLOTINS

Once called 'Little Black Boys,' these characters portray the African slaves who did everything they were told to do by the planter. In this case, they do the bidding of Papa Djab, mainly collecting money from onlookers and responding to his chants. They are mischievous imps and their main aim is to dirty the clothes of onlookers by rubbing against them as they pass.

In days of old, the characters would use molasses to paint their bodies black. Nowadays, they use body paint or a mixture of crushed coal with Vaseline and are bareback with black tights and/or black shorts. Their lips are painted red with fake blood coming from their mouths (a modern addition).

The Ti Djabs collect money thrown to them on the street and bring to Papa Djab for his money pouch. They also follow Acrobat when he teases Mary Anset which results in one of the dramatic rituals on the street. As a matter of fact, the Ti Djabs are also "killed" and revived in both Rituals. Characters may number from 4 to 8 and are all males.

Tip: To remove body paint or Vaseline and coal mixture, rub sand all over and bathe in the sea. Take a shower when you get home but for at least one week, do not sleep on sheets or pillowcases.

Traditional Masquerade of Saint Lucia

MARY ANSET

Translation: Pregnant Mary

This character is the slaves' portrayal of Mary, the pregnant mother of Jesus, in the European story of the Nativity. She is pregnant and follows Papa Djab around. She makes a specific belly movement to the rhythm of the chants and her interaction with Acrobat and the Ti Djabs is the reason for one of the Rituals.

Mary Anset wears a brightly-coloured dress with a protruding belly, shoes and torn unmatched stockings or socks with holes. She carries a handbag and wears a large hat that partially covers her brightly made-up face. This character is typically played by a male but is the only character that may be played by a female.

KABWIT

Translation: Goat

Kabwit, also known as Black Djab, is a terror-instilling character. Dressed in burlap fabric with face and arms painted black, he is usually barefooted. He wears black horns on his head and carries a long black stick which he swings randomly. In days of old, he would use it to hurt persons who got in his way. Nowadays, he threatens the swing without any contact.

Unlike the other characters, Kabwit stands silently by, seemingly oblivious to what Papa Djab and his entourage are doing, although, if he is within earshot, he may respond to chants. Once the rituals are over, he sings:

"Bonswè nom nou kay donmi.
Bonswè dam nou kay dódó."

Translation:
  Good night men we are going to sleep.
  Good night ladies we are going to sleep.

THE CHANTS

These are the Chants of Papa Djab and his followers. Chants and rituals are mostly in St. Lucian Kwéyòl, the indigenous language of St. Lucia, a combination of African and French languages. Chants have specific rhythmic patterns and take the form of calls mainly by Papa Djab, and are repeated as often as possible. Acrobat may lead one or two chants, the Ti Djabs lead one or two chants, and Kabwit has one chant.

The introductory chant is led by the Ti Djabs. Papa Djab announces himself by shouting "Ohhhhh Langlitèèèè!" pronounced Langleetehhhh, meaning Ohhh England, a form of ridicule as the planters in St. Lucia at that time were British. The response from his entourage is "Mi Djab-la", pronounced Me Jabla, meaning the devil is here or literally, look the devil there.

CHANT AN KWÉYÒL	PHONETIC PRONUNCIATION

1. CALL: *Woy Woy*   Woy Woy
    RESPONSE: *Mi Djab-la*   Me jab-la

English Meaning:
Woy woy, look the devil there.

This chant introduces the entourage and may be chanted anytime during the performances.

2. CALL: *Bay Djab tizing*   By Jab teezing
    RESPONSE: *Tizing Tizing ankon*   Teezing uhcor

English Meaning:
Give the devil a little something, a little something, a little something again.

This chant is used to ask onlookers for money and is repeated until money is given. Coins are usually thrown in the opposite direction to keep Ti Djabs from getting too close. All money collected is put in Papa Djab's sack.

3. CALL: *Ki lè-y yé*   Keeleh ee yay
    RESPONSE: *Higas*   Heegas

English Meaning:
What time is it? Heegas

With this chant, Papa Djab is announcing that it is time to grab a child. As young children, we would be following Papa Djab until he started this chant, then we would start backing away to look for a safe place to hide.

Traditional Masquerade of Saint Lucia

CHANT AN KWÉYÒL	PHONETIC PRONUNCIATION

4. CALL: *Bay Djab-la manjé an ti manmay* By Jab-la muhjay un tee mamie
   RESPONSE: *Yonn, dé, twa timanmay* Yon day twa tee mamie

English Meaning:
Give the devil a little child to eat, one, two, three little children

This chant signals the hunt for a child to grab.

5. CALL: *Piti Kon Nou Piti* Peetee konoo Peetee

   RESPONSE: *Tralala* Tralala
   CALL: *Sé lanfè nou ka alé* Say lahfeh noo ka alay
   RESPONSE: *Tralala* Tralala

English Meaning:
Little one as you are little, Tralala, It is to hell we are going (we are going to hell) Tralala

This is to instil fear in the child as parade follows Papa Djab with child in hand. At some point he releases the child.

6. CALL: *An piting piting piting* Uh Peeteeng peeteng peeteeng
   RESPONSE: *Bo* Boe

English Meaning:
None, a rhythmic chant

Acrobat does this chant with responses from the Ti Djabs. It usually is the prelude to either the activities to start the rituals or to prepare for *Ki lè-y yé*.

7. CALL: *Bonbè waya wiyé* Borbeh whya weeyay
   RESPONSE: *Bonbè waya wiyé* Borbeh whya weeyay

English Meaning
None, a rhythmic chant

This chant, sung by Papa Djab and echoed by his entourage, was used to tease any policeman they met along the way, as St. Lucia's police, in the early days, were "imported" from Barbados and could not speak Kwéyòl. Once Papa Djab shouted the chant, the Masqueraders would respond then they would all run away as it was almost a crime to speak Kwéyòl to policemen in those days.

6

PAPA DJAB'S DEATH AND RESURRECTION RITUALS

RITUAL 1

(Acrobat and Ti Djabs form a circle and tease Mary Anset, chanting repeatedly)

Acrobat: Mary ka dansé byen hosé

Ti Djabs: Gri gri ah.

Acrobat: (Gets carried away and tries to touch Mary Anset)
(He chants repeatedly) *Voyé dló ba mwen mwen ka bwilé.*

Ti Djabs: *Voyé dló.*

(Chants of Acrobat and the Ti Djabs quicken until they reach fever pitch.)

Papa Djab: (Looks around. When he speaks, it is in a loud angry voice.)
Ohhhhhh langlitèèèèèèèèèè!

Acrobat and
Ti Djabs: *Mi Djab-la.*

Papa Djab: (Lunges angrily towards them and repeats himself multiple times, getting angrier each time)
Jwé épi mwen, pa jwé épi fanm mwen!
(Papa Djab pretends to stab Acrobat and Ti Djabs with his staff until they all "die".)

(Acrobat and Ti Djab fall to the ground with a variation of antics and feign death. Papa Djab paces up and down angrily making evil angry sounds. He then holds his tail and waves it over each individual "dead" character.)

Papa Djab: *Eee griii ahhhh toebahhhhh.*

(Each character revives in his own dramatic style.)

Ti Djabs: (singing repeatedly) *Woy, woy, mi Djab-la.*

Traditional Masquerade of Saint Lucia

RITUAL 2

Acrobat tries to steal Papa Djab's pouch by pulling at it. Papa Djabs reacts each time he tries. Ti Djabs try to defend Papa Djab.

Papa Djab: (gets more and more angry and in a loud voice shouts)
Ohhhhhh langlitèèèèèèèèè!

Ti Djabs: *Mi Djab-la.*

(Papa Djab and Acrobat have a stick fight urged on by the Ti Djabs. Acrobat takes Kawbit's stick from him and uses it in the fight. Papa Djab "kills" Acrobat with his staff and then shocks the Ti Djabs by also "killing" them with his staff. They all die with a variation of antics. Papa Djab then paces up and down angrily with evil angry sounds. He then uses his tail and goes over each individual dead character to revive them.)

Papa Djab: (Repeats over each character.)
eee griii ahhhh toebahhhhh!

(Each character revives in his own dramatic style.)

All, led by Acrobat:
(Repeatedly)
Woy, we want over.
Yes Manman, we want over.

(They then find another location and start the ritual all over again.)

When all is over and the street performance is coming to an end:

Kabwit: (singing)
Bonswè nom nou kay donmi.
Bonswè dam nou kay dódó.

18

INTERESTING FACTS

- St. Lucia's Masquerade tradition is a Christmas tradition, unlike most of the Windward Islands whose Masquerade traditions remain a Carnival tradition.

- Traditional Masquerade is a given at our New Year's Day *Assou Skwè* (pronounced Asoo Square) celebrations, a local fair that takes place at the Derek Walcott Square in Castries.

- Columbus Square was the original name of the Derek Walcott Square and was the early performance area for the Masquerade. The square is named after our second Nobel Laureate, Sir Derek Walcott.

- Most of the buildings around the Square, with the exception of the Roman Catholic Cathedral and the Central Library, were homes with high balconies and verandas.

- Masqueraders performed for their employers many of whom lived in the houses around the Square. They and their friends would gather in the balconies and throw coins to the performers below. This was a source of income for the performers. The change from homes to business houses coupled with the change of Assou Skwè venues helped with the demise of the traditional masquerade in the late 1900's.

- Monkey Hill in Marchand, Cedars and La Pansee in Castries, Goodlands, Cul-de-Sac, Oleon in the Dennery Valley were some of the places from which the Masqueraders came.

- There is a masquerade tradition in the west coast town of Soufriere called "Djab Dèwò."

- Originally, all Masquerade performers were male.

- Pay Bannann was the first female character.

- The wooden frame of the Chouval Bwa, the wooden horse character, was taken from the locally-made, wooden merry-go-round.

- Uncle Sam and his wife Seraphina, the two stilt walkers, were first seen on the streets in the 1900's.

- It is said that Papa Djab is also called Toes because one of the original performers had an abnormality on one of his feet and was nicknamed Toes.

- Papa Djab's trident is red with four fingers; the little finger is not included. There is no record of why one finger is excluded but one suggestion is that it was to demonstrate the original Papa Djab's abnormality.

- Edward, Everton, and Zotèy were three known Papa Djab performers.

- The throwing of coins on the street for the Masqueraders by the audience is a vital part of the performances. It keeps the Ti Djabs away and is a form of income for performers.

ABOUT THE AUTHOR

Daughter of Winville and Thelma King: historian and educator respectively, June is the second child and only daughter, and sibling of her elder brother Winville Junior. From an early age, she was immersed in traditions and culture of her country by her Dad who took her to many of the early quadrilles and cultural activities, and taught her about the wonderful people who practiced the traditions of St. Lucia.

In 1978 she married Robert Frederick of St. Kitts. They have four children, Gabriele, Omari, Darcel and Kareem. Her marriage to Robert, a Banker by profession, took her to Montserrat, St. Vincent, St. Kitts and Nevis, and Antigua. During this time, the 1980's until the early 1990's, she taught high schoolers Caribbean History and Creative Arts.

June Frederick (right) pictured with a member of the YIA Masqueraders of the Youth in Arts (YIA) Theatre Company

On her return to St. Lucia, she worked with the St. Lucia National Trust as Administrative Assistant and created "Festival of Comedy" one of the Trust's main fundraisers as well as a summer programme "Kids Safari Summer," and a Christmas festival entitled "Christmas Folk Fiesta" which highlighted the traditions of Christmas and, more importantly, the traditional Masquerade. After six years with the Trust, she went to the Folk Research Centre as Executive Director for five years. While there she served as Chairperson of the Committee which was responsible for writing St. Lucia's National Cultural Policy and creating its implementing agency, the Cultural Development Foundation. She also started Folk Theatre performances and produced Adrian Augier's *Hewanorra Story* and an-out-of-workshop Production *Bonjou Ma Titi* directed by Louis McWilliams of Trinidad. As part of the Jubilee Trust Fund Committee created by Monsignor Patrick Anthony to fund projects for the Arts and the Poor, she was associated with the production of *Sarafina* which was staged sixteen times with a cast of over thirty youngsters.

One of her most memorable projects at Folk Research Centre was one to document traditional Masquerade in St. Lucia, Dominica, and St. Kitts and Nevis with the assistance of UNESCO's Alwin Bully and the late Patricia Charles. For St. Lucia, this project was also the beginning of the drive to revive the folk form. Her love for Masquerade continued even after she left Folk Research Centre, and she continues to promote traditional arts and teach Masquerade to schools and youngsters.

In 2000, KiddiCrew.com was born, first as a television programme with Fimber Anius (now deceased), then branching out into KiddiCrew Travel Club, KiddiCrew Summer Fun, KiddiCrew Theatre Company and in 2010, KiddiCrew Project Masq' Camp (teaching traditional Masquerade to children) which

About the Author

trains students of primary school, Theatre Arts classes of secondary schools, and other community groups during November and December, and culminates in traditional street parades.

June also became an avid pan player and eventually leader of Allegro Pan Groove, an all-female steelband group which staged one of the first steelband musicals and children's Pan workshops, participated three times in the local Panorama competition, and performed in Martinique, Washington and Denmark under her leadership.

In 2009, June produced a children's activity book on the traditional Masquerade of St. Lucia entitled *Piti Kon Nou Piti* as a follow-up to the Masquerade revival project done with Folk Research Centre. The sale of books is also used annually to raise funds for the work on teaching traditional masquerade in schools and annual street performances.

June formed a street performing Masquerade group, YIA Masqueraders, with members of the Youth in Arts (YIA) Theatre Company in 2015. The group performs mainly during the traditional Christmas season, and one of the two sections of the group also performs at private functions during the year. She wrote her first children's activity book with DVD on the Traditional Masquerade of St. Lucia in 2009 and also teaches the traditional Masquerade to schools, institutions and private groups. In 2020, June created a Blog page "culturecornerstlucia.com" where she uses the origins of St. Lucia's traditional Masquerade to teach the history, culture and traditions of St. Lucia.

From 2013 to 2016 and again in 2018 June, created and managed a children's summer programme entitled Youth Summer Arts Platform for the Cultural Development Foundation, that included developing skills in creative writing, script writing, and the performing Arts, and at the end of each four-week programme, staged a major production. All productions have been based on one or more Caribbean traditions. The last was not a staged performance but a film on the history of St. Lucia.

In 2015 KiddiCrew Theatre Company was formed to stage one major annual Production featuring the work of St. Lucian playwrights. The Theatre Company, which changed to Youth in Arts (YIA) Theatre Company in 2016, has staged the work of late playwright Roderick Walcott, featuring the music of Charles Cadet for three consecutive years until 2017 and in 2018 staged the work of Drenia Frederick, a young St. Lucian playwright. These productions have introduced youngsters to the life and work of the late Roderick Walcott along with upcoming St. Lucian playwrights and have encouraged the appreciation of our traditions as their work covers St. Lucia's exciting cultural landscape.

June's passions are simple…development of youngsters in the Arts and traditional Masquerade. She passionately believes that the Arts provide invaluable disciplines for life while providing youngsters with skills for Theatre, and that learning about one's culture and participating in traditional Arts instills a sense of national pride that nothing else can teach.

She thanks her wonderful parents for her happy positive childhood full of learning and fun for directing her paths. June is a recipient of the St. Lucia Medal of Merit Gold and Rotary International's Paul Harris Fellow for her outstanding work in Arts and Culture in St. Lucia.

June Frederick (back row third from the left) pictured with the YIA Masqueraders of the Youth in Arts (YIA) Theatre Company

ABOUT THE ARTISTS

ALWYN ST. OMER

Born at Castries, Saint Lucia in 1958, Alwyn St. Omer was inspired by the work of his father, the late Sir Dunstan St. Omer a widely acclaimed international artist of Saint Lucian origins and by his mother Cynthia, a secretary in the Prime Minister's office. She encouraged him by providing a regular supply of art materials.

Alwyn was also inspired by the plentiful supply of picture books around the house and at about age six, was introduced to comics, including the Illustrated Classics, which fueled his appetite, not only for graphic design, but also for folktales and storytelling in a pictorial format. Growing up in an artistic environment with nostrils tuned to oil paints, provided further stimulus.

As a young aspiring artist Alwyn was also privileged to witness plays performed by a famous local theatrical company, the Saint Lucia Arts Guild, adding a dimension of realism to what he saw and read in the comics. He was enamoured by plays steeped in the island's rich folk and musical traditions that included some of the early works of the island's Nobel Laureate, poet Derek Walcott and his playwright, twin brother Roderick.

It is from this launching pad that young Alwyn, budding artist and storyteller, was thrust into orbit, a creative artist with very deep passion and lifelong desire to document his island's cultural heritage through his drawings and paintings. For him, rediscovery and preservation of all the treasures forming the formidable expanse loosely termed Saint Lucian folklore would be his life's achievement. Its art, myths, writings and traditions, its National Theatre, all housed in one monumental edifice.

Alwyn studied Art at the Edna Manley School for Visual Arts in Jamaica and Video production and Audio Visuals at Portsmouth College in England. His work includes the design of Saint Lucia's National Independence Monument and the "Moon Dancer" Masquerade series of paintings. This series is an attempt, in painting, to revive interest in and to Save the lost Masquerade tradition, as a medium to acknowledge the islands rich biodiversity and to promote the concept for the preservation of our natural and cultural heritage. He is a Director of the St. Omer Art Institute, and has a list of publications under his belt, including Sands Tourism Magazine, the CIMPEX Home Companion Magazine, and the Wakonté series of children's colouring books and comics. He is also former television producer and carnival band leader and designer. As a painter, Alwyn also specializes in abstract art, landscape paintings and murals.

Mr. St. Omer's paintings appear in this book on the front and back cover, in the Masqueraders on the title page, and on page 8.

About the Artists

JONATHAN GUY-GLADDING

Jonathan Guy-Gladding (JAG) first came to Saint Lucia as a Peace Corps Volunteer in 1999. Originally from Cape Cod, Massachusetts, he had been working as a computer artist and animator for Sesame Street in New York City—a dream job, but after five years he felt the urge to broaden his horizons and make a greater contribution to the world. He applied to the Peace Corps and was sent to Saint Lucia where he was assigned to teach woodworking to teenagers in the village of Laborie. He found there an unending supply of rich subject matter in the faces and postures of the uniformed schoolchildren, the people going about their daily lives, and the traditional cultural aspects that make Saint Lucia such a wonderful and distinctive place. The pride in heritage and Kwéyòl culture combined with a sense of community and responsibility toward one another deeply impressed him and gave direction to his work. So with all these elements set in front of a landscape of vibrant greens, stunning blues, and warm browns, and illuminated by a quality of light he had never experienced before, he found in Saint Lucia what artists have always traveled far and near to find—true inspiration.

He began painting again and decided that when his two-year stint was up he would devote himself to painting full-time. That was more than eighteen years ago and he's been painting full-time ever since and continues to live in Laborie. During those years he has exhibited extensively in the Caribbean, the US, and the UK, and won numerous awards, including first prize at the Cape Cod Art Association's National Exhibition (twice) and Awards of Excellence and Narrative Excellence at The National Oil and Acrylic Painters Society Best of America exhibition. His portrait commissions include two prime ministers and two governors general. He is also the host and co-founder of an annual painting event in Laborie called "Paint the Village."

It is Jonathan's desire to tell a story in details, whether it is about the warmth and spirit of the people of the Caribbean or something as simple as the way the reflected light colors the edge of a child's face. With his art, he endeavors to do his part in preserving what is so special about Saint Lucia and its people, and share with others his sincere love and appreciation for his subject.

Mr. Gladding's paintings appear in this book on Masquerade band on the title page and pages 2, 3, 4, 5, 6, 8, 12, 13, and 14.

Lightning Source UK Ltd.
Milton Keynes UK
UKHW050911041121
393350UK00002B/75